young men dancing

dancing

Linda Chase

Smith/Doorstop Books

Published 1994 by
Smith/Doorstop Books
The Poetry Business
The Studio
Byram Arcade
Westgate
Huddersfield HD1 1ND

ISBN 1 869961 64 1
Typeset at The Poetry Business
Printed by Swiftprint, Huddersfield

The Poetry Business gratefully acknowledges the
help of Kirklees Metropolitan Council and Yorkshire
& Humberside Arts.

Acknowledgements
Thanks are due to the editors of the following publica-
tions in which some of these poems have appeared:
Scratch, *The Poetry Business Anthologies 1993 & 1994*,
Sodem, *The North*, *Iron*.
'In Rural Vermont' won first prize in the Surrey Com-
petition 1993, 'My Father Had Two Coats' was a winner
in the Lancaster Lit Fest Competition 1993 and 'Straw-
berry Bed' was runner up in the Kent and Sussex
Competition 1993.

Linda Chase is an American living in Manchester
where she teaches Tai Chi. She has worked in commu-
nity arts and was the founding editor of *Cahoots*
magazine. She has two grown up children, a degree in
Creative Writing and has published poems in many
British quarterlies.

CONTENTS

for Skip

YOUNG MEN DANCING

Who were those young men dancing?
And why were they dancing with you?
And what was the meaning of all that business
around the area of the pelvis, both pelvises,
I mean, since I saw you with two of them.
Two men, that is, with one pelvis each.
Though there's your pelvis too, to reckon with.
It made quite a show of itself out there
on the dance floor. Not to be overlooked.
Nor slighted in any way, sticking like a magnet
to the erratic rhythms of those young men,
their jeans curving and cupping and making
promises in all directions of things to come.

Which way to go, you must have asked yourself
a dozen times at least, as the young man
with the smile turned this way, and the
young man with the dreamy eyes turned that,
and you were dazed, in circles, spinning
this way and that way, brushing up against them
in confusion, body parts in gentle friction
sliding back and forth, nearly seeming like
you hadn't meant to do it.
Did you mean to do it?

Could they feel your nipples harden?
Did they know what must have happened
as your thighs began to stick together, throbbing
to the music? Thank God there was the music
you could hide behind and make it look like dancing.
I'm wondering just how much attention
young men pay.

THE TAILORESS AND THE GENTLEMAN

If I cut wide enough for the crotch, noticing
carefully on which side to be generous,
and leave an ample gusset for the buttocks,
the cloth can cup around the groin, neither grabbing
nor pulling itself or the gentleman out of shape.
Cloth, by nature has no greed and I would be
mistaken if I let it hug your thighs too tightly
or caused a pucker anywhere from stretching.

Be sure, the cloth would not be blamed and so
I let the pleats fall full and open from your waist
and let the trousers hang quite freely on your legs.
A fine fabric needs to move to be admired and
I shall let the quality of drape be well displayed.

It's excellence I'm offering you, dear sir.
Fine cloth, fine cut, fine fit. It's up to you.
The perfect fit is all and all my pride is in it.

UPROOTING

Uprooting is a subtle and powerful technique of Tai Chi, which, when performed at a high level, seems effortless. The person receiving an uprooting push appears to fly upwards and backwards.

As you can see, I've hardly moved at all
and yet my sparring partner's been uprooted.
He's flying high, about to hit the wall.

You might think it's because he's very small
and that I had him specially recruited.
But you can see, I've hardly moved at all.

I could have demonstrated how a brawl
would make it look as if he had been booted,
flying so high, about to hit the wall.

It might be, he would soar and never fall.
For this, a crane would be much better suited.
And you can see, I've hardly moved at all.

Uprooting is a skill, though you can call
it talent or a blossom which has fruited.
He's flying like a bird, up toward the wall.

On the wall, the fruit tree branches sprawl.
His landing will be broken, soft and muted.
He's flying high, about to reach the wall.
He's on his own, I've hardly moved at all.

DILIGENCE

If I work harder than you,
I mean much harder,
will I do better than you,
I mean much better?
Will I get more than you,
I mean much more?

I want a lot.
I want more than you
because I deserve it.
You know, rewards, fruits,
justice. Weighing it out,
measuring it up, getting the goods.
I want it to balance out, on my side.

I want lots of little gold
stick-on-stars beside my name
and I want you to have just empty boxes
because you sleep late
and dream and eat grapes in bed
and you always want me
to play with you.

IN RURAL VERMONT

I have slipped past a spinning wheel,
a butter churn and a large dog, to sit here
in the bentwood rocking chair beside your bed.
We must be the remains of Early Americans
who look out the windows at bare Maple trees
and the sides of barns through slatted blinds.
Winter, snow, the sound of a car from time to time,
four wheel drive, snow tires whistling on the road.
The houses are close to the road in rural Vermont.
How else would we ever get out in winter?

The New York Times is spread across your chest,
Vermont Courier at your side, brief case, papers.
Beside you, cards, letters, flowers, the telephone.
A glass of water is full, the straw has been renewed.
I wouldn't dream of touching a thing as you sleep.
In the late afternoon, I field a phone call from a friend,
though I'm to wake you if they call from the Court House.
State's rights, Federal law, something about dentists.

The runners of my chair on the braided rug,
rocking, pad the sound of your bound breath.
I'm glad this chair was left so close to the bed.
I wouldn't want to move the furniture to be close to you.
Our mother's quilt is bunched a little at your feet,
but for the life of me, I leave it.

MY FATHER HAD TWO COATS

I didn't exactly take it off him
while his body was still warm.
No, it wasn't like that at all,
though I did eye it up in the closet
for weeks before he died—
in fact for months and years.

It was an uptown coat.
Charcoal cashmere herringbone, outside
and inside, silk with secret pockets hidden
in the lining. The buttons at the cuff
popped up through slitted button holes.
Look how they open and close and let the
cuffs turn up in such a perky way. It's easy
to imagine the business trends he followed
Monday to Friday in the New York Times,
Long Island Rail Road, Port Washington line.

This coat said everything. Now,
when I wear it, it talks to me
and keeps me warm.

In fact, much later, when I saw him
swaddled in white plastic, the kind
you couldn't see through at all,
though it was opened at the neck
and bunched behind his head as
if it were a hood, he was cold.

In places the plastic was taped,
in others, it was tucked like a careless
sheet in a downtown rooming house.
His eyes were closed and his jaw
was wrapped to keep his mouth in place.
How lightweight the covering was,
so like the packaging we use to

bundle up the stuff we throw away.
Just a thin film keeping it all together.

This coat said everything.
It clings to me. I listen.
I'm cold.

HOUSE PAINTER

She painted the front door green
more than seventeen times,
letting it veer towards turquoise
during the middle years.
Aqua Marine, they called it then,
to sound and look like the sea.
Later the green was more like trees.

The chalky white on the outside walls
she painted more than thirty times,
up and down with a long handled brush,
the whitewash drying as fast as it was spread.
It simply got whiter each time.
Brightness building in the narrow passages,
reflecting the walls across the way.

She was there when I passed this morning,
sitting on the steps in the courtyard,
three green figs turning purple in her hand.

THE GLASS ROOM

Leaf shapes cross your face,
trailing patterns of Clematis, Forsythia
and twisted lines of Honeysuckle vines,
as the sun hits the glass room in patches.

It pushes its way through the Chestnut first
and then past the Ash, the Cherry,
the climbers and the shrubs before
it makes its way through the window panes.

Is it the light or leaves which mark your face?
I see the traces of branches on your legs
and the mullions of windows bar your arms.
My eyes keep wandering toward the door.

Everything out there in the garden is on you,
blotched like a life-sized landscape tattoo
laid out in wooden frames held by glass.
You seem to have more markings than skin.

Glass is no protection. We might as well
step straight out into the dappled afternoon.
Out beyond the climbers, the shrubs, the trees.
Beyond the road, far ahead, the pink sky is spotless.

THE REAL THING

You gave me your cap,
well, it was raining, wasn't it?
The red baseball cap you had been wearing all day.
When I first saw you this morning at the airport,
wearing it in the Denver heat,
I had imagined how your head looked under it
without your hair. Even your eyebrows
nearly gone and so suddenly grey
and your cheeks grey too, eyelids and ears like paper.
It was kind of you to wear the cap.
It made a dome over your scalp
catching the air and keeping you cool,
with those little ventilation screens on the sides.
Good for home runs, I suppose.
Designed for pitching and no-hitter.
It wasn't a souvenir.
It was the real thing.

Before, driving higher, getting colder
you had given me the denim jacket
lined with lumberjack plaid. Remember,
you found it on the road, pockets full of marijuana?
And before that, the woollen sweater,
long sleeves, high neck, green and cosy.
And long before that, hiking boots
trekking me beside you into the High Sierras.
And before that, the crash helmet and the lessons to ride,
balancing the motorcycle for me
with your long legs reaching the ground.
And before that, the yellow dress.
You said it looked like the sun.
Well, we were 20 and I never wore anything under it,
brushing against you to arouse myself.
And before that, you gave me California Highways
and blazed trails and Indian woven rugs and books
and frantic fucks on the side of the road

and stories about rattle snakes and forest fires
and harmonicas in aluminum Air Stream trailers
and songs and cigarettes and emergency stops
in motel rooms to fuck some more and bleed and cry
and sing.
And letters and trans-Atlantic phone calls
and trail maps and mountain trips in jeeps
and no-spill coffee mugs
and meetings in San Francisco at dawn.
Street corners, hippie bars, back roads, whiskey
and extra thick mittens for the snow.

So many things.
Decking me out
and turning me on,
opening me up,
then swaddling me
from head to toe
as if you could ever keep me safe.
Here we go! Play ball!
Barrel-assing down the road,
leaning on the lips of cliffs,
diving into snow drifts
when the pass closes.

Today, on this Colorado mountain
in the drizzle, not far from the jeep,
walking just a short distance on the level,
I hear your lungs sucking breath up from your feet.
It is a dry, hollow sound. You cough.
Perhaps I won't have noticed.
Pine needles everywhere,
underfoot, wet, uncertain as sand.
I am completely unprepared.
I take the cap.
How can I refuse?
It's not a souvenir.

EXPATRIATES DREAMING

Blue eyes on a black woman's breast,
black skin on a blue eyed man's crimson bed,
orange patterns dancing on the bedclothes
which now wrap around her slender limbs,
so just one hand is showing near her face,
pink palm turned up, fingers pointing toward the door,
dark blue pillows tucked under the white man's head,
green pyjama bottoms on the rug beside the bed,
the smell of embers, of candle wax, of last night's sex
and of overripe persimmons in a bowl with decoration,
turquoise zig zag darting around the rim
in between big, salmon coloured dots.

I seem to have dreamed the wrong dream by mistake.
It happens sometimes when the house is full.
In the mix up, perhaps you got one of mine.
I've always been partial to the one with the Jewish princess
and the blue eyed boy in Manhattan, a Greenwich Village loft,
bedding by Bloomingdales, nightwear from Sacks,
nicknacks, mostly ethnic from Africa and New Guinea.
Not much in the fruit bowl. By far my favourite dream.
I'd proudly offer it to anyone, especially a blue eyed man,
travelling between continents and sleeping
across the hall from me. Hope you got it.
I think England is the strangest place for over-nights.

DANCING DADDIES

Of these dancing daddies and their
little girls, my daddy will drop out first.
Look how old and frail he is.
The rhythm in his head can hardly find his feet.
Some of the steps are gone and all the power
in his arms has dried into a cardboard cut-out
shape of how a ballroom dancer looks.
He barely remembers to smile,
but I hold him just the same.

Yours is in his prime and he pulsates.
The music leads him everywhere with you.
He twirls you out and pulls you back
and if he turns his head, you follow him.
Your daddy, packed with dances, has
a thousand thoughts of where to put his feet.
Shuffle hop step tap ball change, spring hop.
You can't quite do it with your child's stride,
but you hold him just the same.

My daddy, in this absent minded shuffle,
keeps me clinging to the dance.
Look how my arms are opened out
and my feet are ambling through the steps
as if a child's jig were dancing to itself.
Please, before the music stops, just once
so I can feel the surging of his lead,
will you let your daddy dance with me?
And I'll hold him just the same.

THIGHS

Somebody's husband put his hand on my thigh
which was right out of order, I thought, and I said so.
'Hey! You've got your hand on my thigh!'
I said, but he knew it, he said, and he left it there.

There's so much practice husbands can get
just looking at thighs on trains, in supermarkets,
at PTA meetings, in the dentist's waiting room,
at the swimming pool, in their own beds at home
and at the Saturday School for Ballet and Tap.

Can't husbands tell, without touching,
what thighs actually are and what they're for?
Can't they see with their own naked eyes
where the tops of anyone's knees begin
and the bottoms of everything else ends?

The long and the short of it, the full figured rub,
the case for thighs, opened and closed.
'Hey! You've got your hand on my thigh!'
I said, but he knew it and left it there. I knew too.

WINDOW

This time when the window cleaner
rattled his way, rung by rung,
up his aluminium ladder, whistling,
(just in case anyone needed to be alerted)
I was alone in the bed.

I heard the chamois leather squeak
against the glass and then,
abruptly, the whistling stopped.
He could see my hand and the back of my head.
The curve of my shoulder was showing.
He knew that I wasn't asleep.

You and I hadn't been sleeping, either,
that day when we let the morning slip.
We had sat up in bed and waved
and he had waved back.
It was so simple, the obvious thing to do.

MR. ONE-YEAR

Mr. One-Year-Older-Than-My-Son,
swathed in aftershave, pub smoke and beer,
while placing both of my hands firmly
onto the hard hollow dents of his buttocks
and letting his pelvis tip slightly forward,
whispered, between licks on my ear, feigned thrusts
and the sound of his own breath, quickening,

'You're only young once. Let's do it.
What have you got to lose?'

Weak at the knees, I began to buckle.
My hand holds broke and I let go.
Free falling fast, I dove back half a century,
plunging past all the things I'd lost.
I know, Mr., it's not the sort of question
you expect a woman to answer.
I won't. Don't worry, but thanks for asking.

STRATEGY FOR THE FORTNIGHT HOLIDAY

It's past the middle. What are we to do?
Week one has gone so fast, neither of us
has a clue what's going on. It's true
we aren't rushing in to make a fuss
about each other and we've never said
a thing which borders on romantic lines.
Ecology and War are there instead
of topics of the heart. I have designs
and secret plots I never talked about.
It was too soon to spring them, but I think
it's only fair to tell you now. No doubt
you'll see, week two has pushed me to the brink.
The planet has its needs and so do I.
Let's bite the toxins, baby, fuck and die.

COUNTRY MIX, MANCUNIAN STYLE

Friday night is frantic out in St. Ann's Square
as the Buffalo Boys go round the outside
and the Buffalo Gals go through it on the hop.
        Side, together, close.
        Side, together, close.
        Give your left to your corner
        and a grand right and left.

Funnel through the alley to the Saturday shops
where the King Street fiddler keeps the tune alive
and Sunday waits through a tunnel of arms.
        Hold the brollies high.
        Hold the brollies high.
        Give your right to your partner
        and swing, swing, swing.

The Buffalo Boys go round the outside
of the Buffalo Gals in a four-hand star.
A quick step dance by the Hidden Gem Church.
        Bow to your partner.
        Bow to your corner.
        Monday comes a'sauntering
        up John Dalton Street.

MY LAWN

It was always called my lawn,
given to me in barrow loads of earth,
notched out of a slope between the garden
and the wild part of the woods.
The children helped us scoop
some ground out of the high side,
then load the barrow and wheel it across.

We raked the earth and levelled it
with pegs and string before we packed it,
sidestepping, rhythmic little stomps
like a troop of Russian dancers.
Then the seeds, scattered by the children
in handfuls, mixed with fish-bone and sand.
You tapped it all down with the back of a spade.

On Sunday, I'll see the trees you planted
in my lawn without permission.
Specimen trees, show pieces by now.
Mature, the children say, not needing stakes,
simply planted wherever you fancied.
Mowing must be difficult without straight lines.
Tell me, who do these trees belong to?

WHAT'S A SHIRT BETWEEN FRIENDS?

This waiting would be sweet if I were certain.
I wouldn't care if you showed up or not.
I'll just hang out, be cool and keep my shirt on.

Uncertainty is rather disconcerting
about the final outcome of the plot.
This waiting would be sweet if I were certain.

What happened to old fashioned winks and flirting
and overtures and foreplay? You forgot?
I'll just hang out, be cool and keep my shirt on.

Why not try the telephone for blurting
out how good you are at bonking, hot shot?
This waiting would be sweeter, were I certain.

Don't dilly dally with your juices squirting
willy nilly. Come on, hit the spot.
I'll just hang out, be cool and keep my shirt on.

Hey! My jeans are white, I don't want dirt on
them, I'll simply slip them slightly past the slot.
This waiting has been sweetened now I'm certain
you'll hang out. You can keep your shirt on.

HEDGE CUTTINGS

Hedge cuttings,
those ordinary shorn-off sprigs
of Hawthorn, Privet and new green Beech
have made their way to the wedding
poking up between the Sweet Peas
in the bride's bouquet.
They give shape, structure and let the
Sweet Peas stand up and look white.
Without them, the flowers
might simply blend into the dress
and not be seen, or later, into the sheets,
or even later, into the white kitchen walls.
We need these occasional markers,
like conifers in suburbs ,
Oaks, intermittent in meadows,
the Great Wall of China from the moon.
We can point and say,
'There it is, over there
beside that thing.' Otherwise
there would be no need at weddings
and we could put our hedge cuttings
directly onto the compost heap.

LUNCH IN LEVENSHULME

The pickles were the best part,
right from the jar, dripping a bit
on the newspapers and leaflets
strewn on the kitchen table.
No need to use a fork, I said.
My fingers fit inside and I can
pull one out for each of you.
The vinegar made our lips sting
and both of them wanted more than one.
But the sandwiches and spinach parcels
neatly wrapped in filo dough
were eaten only by us who had brought
them from the deli, stopping on the way.
No, he said, I've had a snack already
and a snooze, sat here in front of the TV
after I'd done a morning's work in the studio.

My David, he said more than once, as he stroked
the polished features of his son, carved into
mammoth chunks of wood. His house was full of
Davids, other carvings, drawings, mirrors,
paintings, posters, right up to the ceiling.
Then David offered me an almond slice.
You must, he said, eat this.
It's the best thing the deli has to offer.
And so it was. David and I ate everything.
What more could we want?

Before we left, still in the kitchen,
his father stood up and
held out his arms to me.
And then again at the inner door
and again at the outer door,
so full of art and appetites.
A joy to me, he said, again and again.
My son is a joy.

SHOWERING FOR SHABBAS

'Just in the shower,'
you called through the door
and then you flung it open.
'I'm going to my auntie's for dinner.
You caught me just in time.'
Or just too soon, I thought.
You, showering on Shabbas, or just before,
with the bathroom door wide open into the hall.
I wasn't to know when I called on you
with a letter delivered to me by mistake.
Easily done, and fairly often too, since
we are at nearly the same address.

One hand was pushing your hair,
dripping, out of your eyes.
The other held the towel in the crucial place,
as if resting on someone else's fist.
It hung in one long drape, down between your legs,
more like the leaf of a banana, I thought, than a fig.
Your skin, hot and pink, so strikingly arrayed,
with nipples and swirls of rich black hair
thickening on your tummy toward your groin.
Like fur, I thought, between fingers.
Buttocks higher than I had thought
with deep side dents for hands to fit,
I thought, then dropping my eyes
to the puddle spreading around your toes.

Not far from here, your auntie
is getting the table set.
The wine, the candles, the bread.
To be on the safe side,
she probably keeps your yamulka
at her house.
'Oh, a letter for you,
I nearly forgot.'

STRAWBERRY BED

Ever since you put your baby daughter in my bed
to let her sleep, I know whatever follows will follow easily.
Your hand, under the pillow to help lift her head,
your legs as you sit, side-saddle on the edge of the bed
and stretch your arms across to tuck the covers in.
Your stubbled cheek brushing along the pillow
as you bend over her, nestling your face down
close beside hers to plant a goodnight kiss.

She sleeps through all of this as you tell me
that you like the sheets, patterned with strawberries
and strawberry leaves and the smell of the sheets
and the fresh air coming in through the open window.

RETURN OF THE INSECTS

The box I have for keeping insects in
has filled with creatures Linny never knew.

Wood lice, maggots, midges, bed bugs, fleas,
have settled in and crammed the corners up.

'Where can we keep the ones I used to know?'
She tugs my sleeve, 'So, where?' she nags at me.

The temper of this little girl reminds
me I've been cheated out of keepsakes too.

She grabs the box and holds it high until
she drops it when the sparks begin to fly.

The lady bug has flown back to her home.
The fire fly appears, then disappears.

Our house is on fire, Linny.
You are the child, burned.